D1312478

Nellie Bly

History Maker Bios

Shannon Knudsen

⌐ LERNER PUBLICATIONS COMPANY • MINNEAPOLIS

Illustrations by Tim Parlin

Lerner Publications Company
A division of Lerner Publishing Group
241 First Avenue North
Minneapolis, MN 55401 U.S.A.

Website address: www.lernerbooks.com

Library of Congress Cataloging-in-Publication Data

Knudsen, Shannon, 1971–
    Nellie Bly / by Shannon Knudsen.
      p.   cm. — (History maker bios)
    Includes bibliographical references and index.
    ISBN-13: 978–0–8225–2943–9 (lib. bdg. : alk. paper)
    ISBN-10: 0–8225–2943–2 (lib. bdg. : alk. paper)
    1. Bly, Nellie, 1864–1922—Juvenile literature. 2. Journalists—United States—Biography—Juvenile literature. I. Title. II. Series.
    PN4874.C59K68 2006
    070.92–dc22   2004028788

Manufactured in the United States of America
1 2 3 4 5 6 – JR – 11 10 09 08 07 06

TABLE OF CONTENTS

INTRODUCTION

Nellie Bly made her name as a reporter at a time when few newspapers would even hire a woman. She asked bold questions and wrote important, exciting stories. She often wrote about people in need. Her success helped other women follow the same path.

Nellie is best known for one brave deed. In 1889, she rushed off on a thrilling race. She faced storms and sickness to travel around the world faster than anyone ever had. That feat made her the most famous woman in the world.

This is her story.

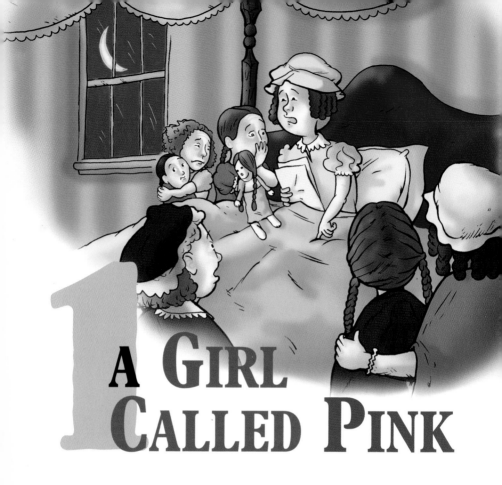

1 A Girl
Called Pink

When Nellie Bly was born on May 5, 1864, her parents named her Elizabeth Jane Cochran. Her hometown shared part of that name. The people of Cochrans Mills, Pennsylvania, had renamed the town for her father years before. Michael Cochran owned a store and a mill and had served as a judge.

Most little girls in the 1860s wore dresses in serious colors such as black or gray. But Mary Jane, Elizabeth's mother, preferred pink for her daughter. Before long, no one called the little girl Elizabeth. They called her Pink.

Pink's father earned plenty of money. In 1869, the Cochrans moved to a huge new house in the town of Apollo, Pennsylvania. Five-year-old Pink had two older brothers and a little sister, Catherine. A little brother, Harry, soon came along too. The big new house had room for everyone.

Most girls, like the ones pictured here, wore dark clothing. But Elizabeth's mother dressed her in pink.

Then a terrible thing happened. In 1870, when Pink was six, her father died. Suddenly, the Cochrans were poor. They had to move to a tiny house two streets away.

Pink missed her father. She found that telling stories was a good way to forget her sadness. She made up fairy tales and love stories for her friends. At night, her mind sometimes got so busy inventing tales that she couldn't fall asleep.

Pink's father built this home in Apollo for the family when Pink was five years old. They had to move one year later.

Apollo, Pennsylvania, in the 1870s was known for its many large, fine homes.

But storytelling couldn't change the fact that her family was very poor. Before long, Mary Jane found a new husband. She hoped that he would help make ends meet. But Jack Ford turned out to be a harsh man who was often drunk. Pink thought that it was terrible for a woman to have to depend on a cruel husband for money. In 1878, Mary Jane divorced Ford.

Pink went to Indiana State Normal School. She hoped to study to be a teacher, but she could only afford one semester.

The family was poorer than ever. Pink decided to train to become a teacher. Then she would be able to support herself and help her mother. But Pink's money soon ran out, and she had to leave the training school.

Mary Jane moved her family to Pittsburgh, Pennsylvania, in 1880. Pink was sixteen, old enough to get married. But after what she'd seen of marriage, she wanted to find another way to live.

Finding work wasn't easy. Young women could be teachers or factory workers, but not much else. For a few years, Pink worked as a tutor and a nanny. She did her best to help Mary Jane take care of the family.

Pink liked to read a newspaper called the *Pittsburg Dispatch*. One day in 1885, she read a piece that made her angry. The writer complained that too many women were working for money. He said that they ought to stay home to care for their families and keep house.

In the late 1800s, Pittsburgh, Pennsylvania, was a growing factory town.

Pink knew that if she and her mother stayed home, the family would go hungry. She wrote an angry letter to the newspaper to make her point. She signed it "Lonely Orphan Girl." The *Dispatch* didn't print the letter. But it did print a notice asking "Lonely Orphan Girl" to come forward and give her name.

A nervous Pink went to the newspaper office and explained who she was. The paper's top editor, George Madden, was a pleasant man. He offered to pay her to write two articles for the *Dispatch*.

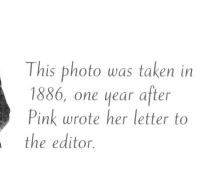

This photo was taken in 1886, one year after Pink wrote her letter to the editor.

Pink could hardly believe her luck. She wrote an article about women's work, then another about divorce. Madden liked her writing. He offered Pink a job for five dollars a week. That was more than a woman could earn in a factory.

Madden wanted Pink to sign her articles with a name that readers would like and remember. He chose one from a popular song by Stephen Foster. From then on, Pink would be known as Nellie Bly.

PEN NAMES

In the late 1800s, few women worked for newspapers. When Nellie started to write for the *Dispatch*, only one other woman worked there. Her name was Elizabeth Wilkinson Wade, but she signed her stories as Bessie Bramble. Some people thought it was improper for a woman reporter to let readers know who she really was.

2 WRITTEN BY NELLIE BLY

Nellie plunged feet first into her new job. She interviewed women who worked in factories. She described the need to plant new trees to keep forests from dying. She told the stories of dancers and musicians. She enjoyed her work, and her readers liked what she had to say.

Nellie had plenty of story ideas. But she was often told to report on clothes, parties, and gardening. The newspaper's editors thought those were proper topics for a woman to write about.

Nellie found most of these subjects dull. She decided to prove that she could write about anything. She would do "something that no other girl has ever done." And she would write about it in a way that editors couldn't ignore.

Nellie liked to write about working women, such those in mills and factories.

Nellie left her job in December 1885, when she was twenty-one. A few months later, she took her mother on a long visit to Mexico City, Mexico. She sent the *Dispatch* stories about the people she met, their customs and foods, and everything else that interested her. Readers enjoyed Nellie's adventures and her funny, spirited way of describing them. Madden hired her back as a reporter when she came home a year later.

The DISPATCH printed Nellie's stories about her travels in Mexico.

In the 1880s, most newspaper jobs were held by men. The newspapers in New York City didn't want to hire Nellie.

This time, Madden told Nellie to write about music and theater. That was better than writing about clothes. But soon, Nellie was bored again. In May 1887, she moved to New York City, home of the most popular newspapers in the world.

Nellie wanted to work for the *World*. This paper ran exciting stories with bold illustrations. Its reporters were the best in the business. But the *World* said no when Nellie asked for a job. So did all the other newspapers she visited.

To Nellie, New York City seemed the best place for a reporter to work.

Nellie kept trying. But after four months in New York, she had no job and almost no money left. Then she lost her purse and all her money with it.

The time had come for action. Nellie went to the office of the *World*. She told the staff that she had an amazing story idea. If they didn't allow her to see an editor, she said, she would take her idea to another newspaper!

The bluff worked. She got to meet the top editor, John Cockerill. She must have impressed him. A few weeks later, she had her first story assignment.

Many New Yorkers had been asking questions about how the city cared for people who were mentally ill. These people were shut away in hospitals and often never seen again. The treatment they received was said to be harsh and unhealthy.

In New York, mentally ill women were sent to Blackwell's Island for treatment.

Until Nellie went inside the hospital on Blackwell's Island, no one really knew how the patients were being treated.

The *World* sent Nellie to discover the truth in an unusual way. She pretended to be insane. Her act was so good that she was sent to a hospital for mentally ill women.

Nellie found that the patients had few warm clothes. The food tasted terrible. The nurses beat some patients, teased others, and gave everyone ice-cold baths. Worst of all, the patients had to sit all day long on hard benches. They weren't allowed to talk, read, or even move. Some of the patients didn't even seem to be mentally ill.

Nellie thought that this treatment was bad enough to make a healthy person go insane. That's exactly what she wrote when the *World* arranged for her to be released from the hospital. After her stories appeared, the city gave more money to the hospitals so that they could improve their care.

Nellie kept reporting. Some of her stories were serious, while others were just for fun. Her personality seemed to charm the people she interviewed. They often told her things that they would never tell another reporter.

FAIR REPORTING

Most modern newspaper reporters wouldn't pretend to be someone they aren't. Lying to get information for a story is seen as unfair and dishonest. But in Nellie's time, no one minded. In fact, readers admired the way she fooled people to get her story. So did the editors of other newspapers. They began to send women reporters on secret assignments like Nellie's.

The more Nellie wrote, the more fans she earned. She loved the excitement of her work and the thrill of having her name known. Best of all, she made enough money to support her mother, sister, and niece.

Still, Nellie wasn't satisfied. She wanted to do something truly unusual, something that no one would ever forget. One day in the fall of 1888, an idea came to her. She would travel around the world faster than anyone ever had.

3 AROUND THE WORLD

The idea of a person rushing around the world as quickly as possible wasn't new. In 1873, French writer Jules Verne had captured readers' imaginations with his book *Around the World in Eighty Days*. In Verne's story, a character called Phileas Fogg circles the globe in record time to win a bet.

A Risky Trip

Nellie was secretly nervous about going around the world. The trip would be dangerous. She would have to travel through bad weather. Her ship might sink, or she might catch a strange disease. She could become stranded in another country. But she was much too determined to let her fears stop her from going.

Fogg's trip was imaginary. In the days before cars and airplanes, no one had ever gone around the world in just eighty days. That was why Nellie was so sure that her adventure would help sell newspapers. Everyone would want to read about such a journey. Nellie's editors agreed, but they wanted to send a man.

Nellie argued that she should be the reporter to go on the trip. But her editors doubted whether a woman could travel alone. It wouldn't be proper. And wouldn't a woman need trunks and trunks full of clothes?

Nonsense, Nellie said. She was comfortable traveling alone. She would take only a single small bag. If the *World* wanted to send a man, she said she would go anyway and would finish before him. The *World* decided to send Nellie.

With her checkered coat and small bag, Nellie was ready to take off on her trip around the world.

Her adventure began when she sailed for Great Britain from New Jersey on November 14, 1889. She was twenty-five years old. In order to break Phileas Fogg's record, she would have to be home by February 2, 1890.

Right away, the rocking of the ship made Nellie seasick. She got used to ocean travel, though. After six days at sea, she reached Great Britain. Nellie hurried on to France, where she met Jules Verne. He wished her well, and off she raced to Italy by train.

Nellie met Jules Verne, the author of AROUND THE WORLD IN EIGHTY DAYS, when she was in France.

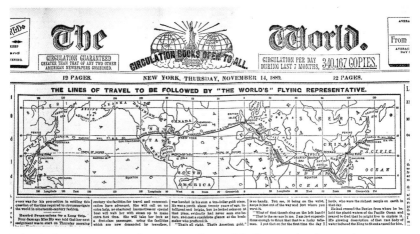

The World.

CIRCULATION GUARANTEED GREATER THAN THAT OF ANY TWO OTHER AMERICAN NEWSPAPERS COMBINED.

CIRCULATION PER DAY DURING LAST 7 MONTHS, 340,167 COPIES.

12 PAGES. NEW YORK, THURSDAY, NOVEMBER 14, 1889. 12 PAGES.

THE LINES OF TRAVEL TO BE FOLLOWED BY "THE WORLD'S" FLYING REPRESENTATIVE.

The WORLD printed stories about Nellie and where she was on her voyage around the world.

Back at home, the editors of the *World* printed as much as they could about Nellie's trip. She could only send a story when she had time and only by a slow method called cabling. Sometimes the *World* had to simply print reports about the places she was visiting. Still, thousands of people bought the paper to find out how Nellie was doing.

From Italy, Nellie sailed to Egypt. Everywhere she went, she saw things and people that she'd never seen before. Merchants, beggars, and magicians became parts of the stories she wrote for the *World.*

These Americans in Tokyo, Japan, are enjoying rickshaw rides like the one Nellie had in Colombo.

Nellie was two days ahead of schedule when she got to Ceylon, an island south of India that is now called Sri Lanka. But her next ship was late leaving. She had to wait five slow days. She toured the city of Colombo, drank delicious tea, and took a ride in a rickshaw, a cart pulled by a man.

At last, her ship left for Singapore, an island in the South China Sea. There, she bought a pet monkey and named it McGinty. Nellie reached Hong Kong on December 23. Her ship had sailed so quickly that she was ahead of schedule again.

When Nellie went to the shipping company's office, she received bad news. Nellie wasn't alone in her quest. A magazine called *Cosmopolitan* had also sent a woman reporter to break Phileas Fogg's record. Her name was Elizabeth Bisland, and she was a few days ahead of Nellie. Even worse, Nellie would be stuck in Hong Kong for five days, waiting for her next ship. Her grand adventure was at risk of turning into a failure.

4 THE MOST FAMOUS WOMAN

Nellie decided that Elizabeth Bisland didn't matter. Nellie's race was against time, not another reporter. She spent her days in Hong Kong sightseeing. She had started to feel homesick, though. She spent Christmas at a Chinese temple, feeling lonely. She was glad to leave for Japan.

In Japan, Nellie saw beautiful Japanese dancers. She also enjoyed a lunch in her honor on a U.S. Navy ship.

The *Oceanic*, Nellie's last ship, set out across the Pacific Ocean on January 7, 1890, headed to San Francisco, California. Nellie had less than four weeks to finish her journey. The crew of the *Oceanic* was excited to have her aboard and wanted to help her win the race.

The OCEANIC carried Nellie across the Pacific Ocean, back to the United States.

At first, the *Oceanic* kept up a fast pace on the way to San Francisco, California. But then a huge storm hit and lasted for more than a day. The ship was caught in big waves and moved very slowly.

Nellie started to lose hope. She decided that if time ran out, she wouldn't go back to New York at all. She would be too ashamed.

MONKEY LUCK

The crew of the *Oceanic* didn't like Nellie's pet monkey, McGinty. During the storm that slowed down the trip, McGinty tried to bite one of the ship's workers. Some sailors thought he was bad luck and wanted to toss him overboard. Nellie wouldn't let them.

In the late 1800s, trains were the fastest way to travel over land.

The storm finally passed. Nellie reached San Francisco on January 20. She thought she had plenty of time to finish her trip by train. But the worst snowstorm in ten years had buried the train tracks. Workers would need at least a week to clear the train's path.

This time, the *World* came to Nellie's rescue. The paper paid for a special train to take her south, around the snow-covered tracks.

As the train raced through the southwestern United States, Nellie realized that she was going to succeed. She also learned that Elizabeth Bisland had fallen behind in her trip.

In every city where the train stopped, cheering crowds shouted a welcome to Nellie Bly. Her mother joined her in Philadelphia, Pennsylvania. Together they arrived in Jersey City, New Jersey, on January 25, 1890. Nellie had traveled almost twenty-two thousand miles in seventy-two days, six hours, eleven minutes, and fourteen seconds. She had beaten Phileas Fogg's record by eight days!

Crowds met Nellie at Jersey City and the end of her trip around the world. Newspaper illustrators recorded the scene.

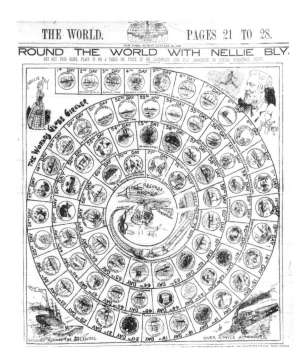

The Nellie Bly
board game,
AROUND THE
WORLD WITH
NELLIE BLY

Nellie's success made worldwide news.
Everyone knew who she was. A woman's
hat and a board game were named for her.
Her image appeared in ads for all sorts of
products. Nellie was still only twenty-five
years old, but she had become the most
famous woman in the world.

When Nellie returned to the *World* after
the trip, she was shocked. The newspaper
didn't give her a raise. They didn't offer her
any kind of reward for her amazing feat.
Her stories had been great for business, but
she got almost no thanks.

Angry, Nellie left her job at the *World*. But she soon found that she couldn't earn a living without reporting. She returned to her job in 1893.

One of her most interesting assignments took her to Chicago, Illinois, in July 1894. George Pullman's railroad workers were on strike. They had stopped working because they were unhappy with their wages. With the workers on strike, the trains couldn't run.

President Grover Cleveland sent soldiers to try to get the trains moving again. Some of the strikers responded by turning over train cars and starting fires. Soldiers fired into the crowd and killed four workers.

Nellie came to Chicago angry about the strike. How could the workers do such things? She was eager to write about it.

Federal troops guard a train engine in Chicago, Illinois, during the Pullman Strike of 1894.

But when Nellie met the workers in person, she changed her mind. She learned that the workers had to live in cramped, dirty apartments owned by George Pullman. He had cut their wages to save money for himself. But he did not cut the rents he charged. Pullman was rich—and getting richer.

Nellie was outraged to see the children of hardworking people going without clothes and shoes because of one man's greed. She was the only reporter who told the workers' side of the story. Her articles didn't change the way the strike turned out. It ended without any gains for the workers. But Nellie helped her readers understand that the workers were real people who simply wanted to take care of their families.

5 MORE WORK TO DO

Less than a year after the Pullman strike, Nellie surprised everyone she knew by getting married. Her husband was a wealthy businessman named Robert Seaman. Nellie was thirty years old. Robert was seventy. For a while after her marriage, Nellie kept reporting. Then, in 1896, the couple traveled to Europe and spent three years there.

THE IRON CLAD FACTORIES ARE THE LARGEST

Of their kind and are owned exclusively by

✳ NELLIE BLY ✳

The only woman in the world
personally managing
Industries of such a magnitude

NATIONAL BOTTLERS' CONVENTIO
CLEVELAND, OHIO
OCTOBER 15, 16 and 17, 1901

Nellie became the president of one of her husband's companies. She did not let it bother her that women did not usually run businesses at that time.

Back at home, Nellie learned about Robert's biggest business, the Iron Clad Manufacturing Company. The company made many kinds of iron goods, from milk cans to kitchen sinks. Nellie became president of the company in 1899. She claimed to be the only woman running such a large, complicated business.

Robert died in 1904. Over time, the Iron Clad began to have serious money troubles. Some of Nellie's workers were stealing from the company. By the time she found out, she couldn't save the Iron Clad. It went out of business in 1911.

Nellie needed a change. In 1914, she traveled to Vienna, Austria. While she was there, World War I broke out. At the age of fifty, Nellie became a war reporter. She traveled to the front lines of battle and sent stories to the *New York Evening Journal.*

FAIRNESS TO WORKERS

Nellie tried to give her workers at the Iron Clad a fair deal. She paid them well. At her factory, she provided a gym, a bowling alley, and a library that the workers could enjoy on their breaks. The factory also had a small hospital in case anyone got sick or had an accident on the job.

NELLIE BLY "ON THE JOB"

*Nellie Bly,
reporting for the
EVENING JOURNAL*

Nellie returned to the United States in
1919, the year after the war ended. In need
of money, she took a reporting job with the
Evening Journal. She used her stories to tell
readers about poor families in need. Many
times, she wrote about children who
needed homes. Some of those children
were adopted because of Nellie's work.
And one little girl, a six-year-old named
Dorothy, came to live with Nellie in 1921.

Nellie's health had begun to suffer. She still worked hard, but in January 1922, she had to go to a hospital. She died there at the age of fifty-seven. (Her young friend, Dorothy, went to live with a kind couple who adopted her.)

Newspapers all over the United States printed notices of Nellie's death. They told the story of her bold life and her many accomplishments. Just as she had planned, Nellie Bly had done things "that no other girl had ever done."

TIMELINE

NELLIE BLY WAS BORN ON
MAY 5, 1864.

In the year . . .

1869 Nellie's family moved to Apollo, Pennsylvania.

1870 her father died. `Age 6`

1879 she tried to become a teacher.

1880 she moved to Pittsburgh, Pennsylvania.

1885 her first newspaper article was published. `Age 21`

1886 she traveled to Mexico and wrote about her experiences.

1887 she moved to New York City.
she posed as an insane person to learn about the care in mental hospitals.
she became a reporter for the *New York World.*

1889 she left on a trip around the world.

1890 she set a record for around-the-world travel. `Age 25`

1894 she covered the Pullman workers' strike in Chicago.

1895 she married Robert Seaman.

1899 she became president of the Iron Clad Manufacturing Company. `Age 35`

1904 her husband died.

1911 the Iron Clad went out of business.

1914 she traveled to Austria and reported on World War I. `Age 50`

1919 she used her writing to help find homes for children.

1922 she died in New York City. `Age 57`

THE NELLIE BLY GUESSING MATCH

Nellie's trip around the world became a contest among more than 500,000 people. The *World* started the Nellie Bly Guessing Match to keep readers interested in Nellie's progress. The paper asked readers to guess how long the trip would take. The closest guesser would win a vacation to Europe and $250.

So many people entered the contest that the *World* had to hire someone just to keep track of the entries. The winner

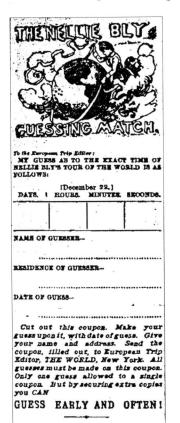

was F. W. Stevens of New York, who guessed the correct time within a second! The newspaper also printed the names of 116 people who guessed within fifteen seconds of the correct time.

FURTHER READING

FICTION

Blos, Joan W. *Nellie Bly's Monkey: His Remarkable Story in His Own Words.* New York: William Morrow, 1996.
McGinty the monkey tells how he traveled with Nellie from Singapore to New Jersey in this amusing picture book.

NONFICTION

Englart, Mindi Rose. *Newspapers from Start to Finish.* Woodbridge, CT: Blackbirch Press, 2001. Find out how newspapers are made, from reporting to layout to printing.

Streissguth, Tom. *Science Fiction Pioneer: A Story about Jules Verne.* Minneapolis: Carolrhoda Books, Inc., 2000.
This life story of Jules Verne includes the creation of *Around the World in Eighty Days*, the book that inspired Nellie's trip.

WEBSITES

The American Experience: Around the World in 72 Days
http://www.pbs.org/wgbh/amex/world/
This is the website of a PBS show about Nellie's career and trip around the world. Visitors can view a map of Nellie's travels and read her writing.

National Women's Hall of Fame—Nellie Bly
http://www.greatwomen.org/women.php?action=viewone &id=23
A brief biography of Nellie explains why this organization has honored her as one of the greatest women in U.S. history.

SELECT BIBLIOGRAPHY

Around the World in 72 Days. A Nebraskans for Public Television, Inc., production for *The American Experience.* PBS Home Video, 1997. Videocassette.

Beasley, Maurine H., and Sheila J. Gibbons. *Taking Their Place: A Documentary History of Women and Journalism.* Washington, DC: American University Press, 1993.

Fredeen, Charles. *Nellie Bly: Daredevil Reporter.* Minneapolis: Lerner Publications Company, 2000.

Kroeger, Brooke. *Nellie Bly: Daredevil, Reporter, Feminist.* New York: Times Books, 1994.

Marzolf, Marion. *Up from the Footnote: A History of Women Journalists.* New York: Hastings House Publishers, 1977.

Mills, Kay. *A Place in the News: From the Women's Pages to the Front Page.* New York: Dodd, Mead and Company, 1988.

INDEX

Acknowledgments

The images in this book are used with permission of: © Museum of the City of New
York, p. 4; Minnesota Historical Society, p. 7; The Apollo Memorial Library, pp. 8, 9;
Special Collections, University Library, Indiana University of Pennsylvania, Indiana,
Pennsylvania, p. 10; © Brown Brothers, p, 11; Carnegie Library, Pittsburgh, pp. 12, 40;
Slater Mill Historic Site, Pawtucket, Rhode Island, p. 15; Library of Congress, pp. 16,
19 (LC-USZ62-22328), 25 (LC-USZ62-59924), 28 (LC-B2-2025-15), 31 (LC-D4-9176),
33 (LC-USZ62-72119), 34 (LC-USZ61-2126), 35 (LC-DIG-ppmsca-02918); © Hulton
Archive/Getty Images, pp. 17, 36; © Photo Collection Alexander Alland, Sr./CORBIS,
p. 18; © Bettmann/CORBIS, p. 20; The Illustrated London News, p. 26; © Collection of
the New York Historical Society (53151), p. 27; © SuperStock, Inc./ SuperStock, p. 37;
Harry Ransom Humanities Research Center, The University of Texas at Austin, p. 42;
General Research Division, New York Public Library, Astor, Lenox, and Tilden
Foundation, p. 45.

Front cover image: Library of Congress (LC-USZ62-75620)
Back cover image: Library of Congress (LC-D4-9176)

For quoted material: pp. 15 and 43, *Pittsburg Commercial Gazette*, January 25,
1890, 1:7, quoted in Brooke Kroeger, *Nellie Bly: Daredevil, Reporter, Feminist*
(New York: Times Books, 1994).